BIRTHDAY BOOK DONATED TO MCAULIFFE LEARNING CENTER BY

TYLER TEBO

AUGUST 26, 2004

The Kids Book of
The Far North

WRITTEN BY
Ann Love & Jane Drake

ILLUSTRATED BY
Jocelyne Bouchard

KIDS CAN PRESS

Dedication
To Charles Drake and Henry Barnett, lifelong friends and scientists —
one a navigator and the other an adventurer, two men who love the wild

Acknowledgments

To write this book, the authors drew on the expert scientific and traditional knowledge
of many Northerners and people who love the North. We extend a special thanks to Dr. Pete Ewins and
Dr. Rolph Davis for reading drafts of the manuscript and for offering countless suggestions and details to better it.
Thank you also to Valerie Hussey, Linda Biesenthal, Julia Naimska and all the creative,
hardworking people at Kids Can Press.

The illustration of John Torrington on page 15 is based on photographs taken by Owen Beattie and published in
Frozen in Time: The Fate of the Franklin Expedition by Owen Beattie and John Geiger (Douglas & McIntyre).

Kids Can Press acknowledges the financial support of the Ontario Arts Council,
the Canada Council for the Arts and the Government of Canada,
through the BPIDP, for our publishing activity.

Published in Canada by
Kids Can Press Ltd.
29 Birch Avenue
Toronto, ON M4V 1E2

Published in the U.S. by
Kids Can Press Ltd.
4500 Witmer Estates
Niagara Falls, NY 14305-1386

Edited by Linda Biesenthal
Designed by Julia Naimska
Printed in Hong Kong by Wing King Tong Company Limited

CM 00 0 9 8 7 6 5 4 3 2 1

Canadian Cataloguing in Publication Data
Love, Ann
Kids book of the Far North

Includes index.
ISBN 1-55074-563-8

1. Arctic regions — Juvenile literature. 2. Arctic peoples — Juvenile literature.
3. Human ecology — Arctic regions — Juvenile literature. I. Drake, Jane. II. Bouchard, Jocelyne. III. Title.

G614.L68 2000   j909'.0913   C99-933011-X

Kids Can Press is a Nelvana company

CONTENTS

THE TOP OF THE WORLD

For nearly half the year, it's dark, extremely cold and very windy in the Far North. In some places, the sun sets in October and doesn't rise above the horizon until February. Winter temperatures can nose-dive below -40°C (-40°F), and fierce winds can blow for days and even weeks. But around the top of the world, plants, animals and people have developed remarkable ways of adapting to one of the harshest climates on Earth. To them, the Far North is home.

Where Is the Far North?
In this book, "the Far North" includes the tree line and everything above it. This remote part of the world is a vast area that covers eight percent of Earth's surface, but includes only a tiny fraction of its people — and all of its 30 000 wild polar bears.

Native peoples of the Arctic know this dangerous but beautiful place like the backs of their hands from traditional knowledge passed down from ancestors who made a home in the Far North thousands of years ago. They share their home with people who moved north to live — some attracted by the North's rich resources, others by its power, beauty and mystery.

Eight countries claim part of the Far North — Canada, the United States (Alaska), Russia, Denmark (Greenland), Norway, Iceland, Sweden and Finland. Recognizing that the Far North is a special but fragile place, people and their governments are cooperating to protect its plants and wildlife, its habitats and the traditional ways of its Native peoples.

Tree Line

The tree line is a border of coniferous trees that zigzags around the top of the world, marking the edge of the Far North's unique ecosystem. Nature draws this line — if the warmest month of the year averages 10°C (50°F) or more, trees will grow. North of the tree line lies tundra, with sparse, miniature plant life, as well as icy barren lands where almost nothing grows.

Arctic Circle

The Arctic Circle is an imaginary line drawn around Earth at 66½° north latitude, 2700 km (1680 mi.) south of the North Pole. At this latitude, the sun doesn't set on the summer solstice, June 21, or rise on the winter solstice, December 21. Some people define the Far North as everything above the Arctic Circle.

North Pole

The geographic North Pole is located near the middle of the Arctic Ocean. The actual spot is not land, but thick sea ice moving over deep water. The nearest land is 725 km (450 mi.) away. The North Pole is located at exactly 90° north latitude, at the point where all the lines of longitude meet. From here, every direction is south.

Magnetic North Pole

In 1831, English explorer James Clark Ross noticed that as he traveled closer to the geographic North Pole, his compass needle bent down. He had found the Magnetic North Pole. At that time, it was 2300 km (1400 mi.) south of the North Pole. Deep inside Earth, liquid metal flows through the core, creating electric currents and magnetic poles at both ends of Earth. Since Ross's time, the position of the Magnetic North Pole has moved to 1500 km (950 mi.) south of the North Pole.

Race to the Pole

For southerners, the most famous spot in the Far North is the North Pole. Many adventurers froze to death searching for it. Americans Robert Peary and Matthew Henson tried seven times before winning the race to the Pole in 1909 with their Inuit guide, Ootah. Peary lost eight toes to frostbite.

ECO WATCH

The Mackenzie River Basin, Bering Strait and Kola Peninsula are considered global hot spots — areas where greenhouse gases from the south are causing average temperatures to rise, melting permafrost, sea ice and glaciers.

Kola Peninsula
FINLAND
Barents Sea
Murmansk
SWEDEN
DENMARK
NORWAY
EUROPE
Bear Island
Norwegian Sea
Svalbard
GREAT BRITAIN
Greenland Sea
ICELAND
Greenland (DENMARK)
ATLANTIC OCEAN
Thule
Baffin Bay
Davis Strait
Baffin Island
Iqaluit
Hudson Bay

▲▲▲▲▲ Tree Line

– – – Arctic Circle

Permanent Ice

IT'S COLD AT THE TOP

The Far North is bitterly cold in winter and cool in summer because it gets only a small share of the sun's heat. In winter, the North tilts away from the sun, creating "polar night" — days of total darkness with average temperatures below -25ºC (-13ºF). The windchill makes it much colder. Exposed skin freezes in less than a minute.

Summer is the brightest time, when the North tilts toward the sun. In June, depending on how far north you live, there's midnight sun and it's light all night long. But the sun is weak, rarely warming the air above 10ºC (50ºF). This is because, close to the poles, the sun's rays must travel through more atmosphere than near the equator. All the snow and ice keep things cool, too. Like an enormous mirror, they reflect the sun's rays away from Earth.

Far North Facts

- The coldest temperature recorded in the North was -70ºC (-94ºF) in Oimyakon, Siberia.

- The coldest windchill factor (combination of temperature and wind speed) ever recorded in the Far North was -92ºC (about -134ºF) in Pelly Bay, Nunavut.

- A covering of 40 cm (15 in.) of snow offers good insulation for creatures that burrow in for the winter. It can be -45ºC (-49ºF) above the snow and -4ºC (about 25ºF) under it.

- Sea smoke and ice fog occur when a mist of ice crystals forms where cold air meets open water. Hunters follow sea smoke to find seals and other sea creatures, but steer around it on their snowmobiles and dogsleds.

- Blizzards, called *purgas* in Siberia, are snowstorms that combine high winds, cold temperatures and reduced visibility. One winter, blowing snow raged for 90 days straight in Resolute, Nunavut.

Children in the Far North learn about cooperation and to respect the wind and cold from stories told by their elders. This is a version of The Wind God's Wife *from the Nenets of Siberia.*

The Wind God's Wife

For many days, a fierce blizzard lashed the tent of an old man and his three daughters. Cold and frightened, the old man said to his eldest daughter, "Kotura the wind god needs a good wife. Go to him. Push your sleigh into the wind and follow it to the hilltop. Then slide down the slope to Kotura's tent. Touch nothing inside, but wait patiently for him. Do exactly as he says and he'll stop the blizzard."

As the eldest daughter set out, a little bird landed on her shoulder. She swatted it away. Once inside Kotura's tent, she greedily ate the last spoonful of stew from his cooking pot.

Kotura arrived home and demanded, "Who are you and why are you here?"

"My father sent me to be your wife," the eldest daughter replied.

"Cook this meat for our supper," demanded Kotura. "Take what is left to my neighbor and bring back the bowl." When she finished eating, the eldest daughter took a bowl of stew and went outside. Blinded by the blizzard, she poured the food on the ground and returned to Kotura.

The next morning, Kotura handed the eldest daughter a pile of reindeer skins. "While I'm hunting, make me boots, mitts and a parka."

The eldest daughter stitched the skins quickly but carelessly. An old woman arrived and pleaded with her, "Help me. I have a cinder in my eye." The eldest daughter snapped at the old woman, telling her to go away. When he returned home, Kotura saw that the clothing was badly sewn and threw the eldest daughter out of his tent.

When the blizzard continued, the old man said to his second daughter, "Your sister has failed. Go to Kotura and save us from the storm." But the old man knew she had also failed when the blizzard raged for another day and night. He turned to his youngest daughter. "Now you must go to Kotura," he said.

The youngest daughter followed the route to Kotura's tent. When a little bird landed on her shoulder, she patted it gently. Once inside the tent, she waited patiently. When Kotura returned home, she prepared a delicious stew. "Take what is left to my neighbor," Kotura told her. Outside, the youngest daughter was blinded by the blizzard until a little bird appeared and showed her the way.

In the morning, Kotura told the youngest daughter to sew him new boots, mitts and a parka. An old woman arrived asking for help, and the youngest daughter removed a cinder from her eye. The old woman pulled four girls from her ear, and together they sewed the clothing. When Kotura returned home, he asked the youngest daughter to marry him.

The old man looked outside his tent. The storm was over. He knew that his youngest daughter was now the wind god's wife.

THE POLAR SKY

People who live in the Far North see the moon and stars in the December daytime sky — but not the sun. Outdoors, they survive bone-chilling cold until the warming sun returns. Even as they shiver, elders watch the sky and remember stories about the stars that brighten their polar winter.

The North Star is located directly above the North Pole, so it doesn't seem to move while the rest of the night sky revolves round it. Old stories from Arctic Europe and Siberia call it the navel of the sky. Some Inuit say that Sila, a powerful spirit of sky and weather, lives there.

On mid-December mornings in the Arctic, the star Altair rises in the northeast. As Earth turns, people in one northern community after another use Altair to time the dawn of their sunless day.

Seven stars dominate the northern sky. People south of the Arctic Circle say they form a big dipper, a plow or a wagon. The ancient Greeks said they formed Artikos, the Great Bear, from which we get the word "arctic." Inuit elders see seven caribou in the seven stars. Siberian elders see a giant reindeer.

From Alaska to Greenland, the Inuit watch stars in the constellations Orion and Taurus and see dogs holding a polar bear at bay while three hunters with a sled run to catch up.

Here Comes the Sun

The sun doesn't rise on December 21 along the Arctic Circle. And the farther north you go, the more sunless winter days there are. When the returning sun finally peeks over the horizon, Inuit elders remember an old taboo — unless children stop playing string games, such as cat's cradle, they might snare the sun's rays and scare it south again.

Six months later, on June 21, the sun doesn't set north of the Arctic Circle. And the farther north you go, the more days of 24-hour sun people enjoy in summer. This midnight sun doesn't shine overhead, but travels in a circle around the sky, just above the horizon.

During the weeks before and after the midnight sun, it is bright enough to read a book outside on a clear night, even though the sun is below the horizon. And for weeks before and after the "great darkness" in winter, the sun doesn't rise, but the southern sky brightens enough to play outdoors at noon.

Sun Dogs

Because the arctic sun is always close to the horizon, its rays can produce amazing special effects. When sunlight passes through ice crystals in the air, a halo may form around the sun or two bright spots, called sun dogs, may appear on opposite sides of the sun.

Northern Lights

Like shimmering green and pink curtains, the northern lights sway across the night sky. A Siberian legend calls them "battling warrior spirits." A story from the Saami people of Arctic Europe says they are dead souls trying to tell the living that summer will return.

People near the North Pole see the northern lights to the south because they are most intense at the latitude of the Magnetic North Pole. Some Northerners swear that, if you whistle, the northern lights will jump closer and make a swishing or crackling sound. Scientists aren't so sure. They say the northern lights are gases high in the atmosphere that glow quietly when struck by tiny particles released from the sun. When more particles than usual reach Earth, the northern lights can be seen far to the south of the Arctic Circle.

THE PREHISTORIC ARCTIC

About 50 000 years ago, Canada's Ellesmere Island was a warm swamp, home to giant trees, ancestral hippos and salamanders as long as crocodiles. But several times between 1.6 million and 10 000 years ago, the Arctic turned much colder than it is now. Massive sheets of ice, called glaciers, formed in the north and then spread south. For thousands of years, most of Canada, the northern United States, Europe and western Siberia were covered with ice up to 3 km (2 mi.) thick.

In an ice age, many glaciers join to form huge ice caps. Scientists think biting winds blew across these caps. The ice inched southward, scraping the land underneath and pushing dirt and rubble ahead like a huge bulldozer. The rumble and groan of the moving ice must have echoed over great distances. Much of Earth's water froze into the ice caps. Sea levels fell and a land bridge formed between Siberia and Alaska.

Beringia

In a few arctic refuges, no glaciers formed. The largest refuge was Beringia, which at times stretched from Siberia's Kolyma River across the Bering land bridge to Canada's Mackenzie River. Beringia remained severely cold, but tundra plants, thick-furred animals and a few human hunters managed to survive there. The Bering land bridge became a corridor for plants, animals and people to cross back and forth between Asia and North America.

The Ice Ages

Earth wobbles slightly as it circles the sun. Some scientists think an ice age is triggered if Earth happens to wobble so the North Pole tilts steeply away from the sun at the same time Earth is taking an unusually long orbit around it.

When the North is that far from the sun's heat, winter snowfalls are greater than summer melts. Old snow becomes packed under new snow until it is pressed into glaciers. Because snow and ice reflect the sun's heat back into space, the glaciers are slow to melt, even after Earth returns to a normal tilt and orbit.

The last ice age ended slowly but sometimes violently. The sun's heat thinned the ice caps before they retreated to the High Arctic. Where

Mammals of Beringia

Ice-age animals didn't spend much time on the glaciers. But in places like Beringia, remarkable mammals thrived despite the severe cold. For those creatures, staying alive meant special adaptations, including thick fur to cut the windchill.

The giant short-faced bear was a head taller than any bear alive today. With unusually long legs, it ran down its prey on cold scrubland.

The woolly mammoth was a long-haired elephant. Using its curved tusks as a snowplow to uncover plants, one mammoth ate mounds of plants every day — enough to fill 25 shopping carts.

The large-horned steppe bison grazed on tundra grasses and was a staple food of early human hunters.

The musk ox — a stocky, longhaired relative of the goat and yak — has survived. When threatened, a herd of musk oxen forms a ring with their young in the center. The adults use their strong skulls and sharp curved horns to keep away predators — even packs of circling wolves.

the ice melted unevenly, vast lakes of meltwater formed behind ice jams and then suddenly burst through, causing catastrophic floods downstream.

When the ice ages ended, wildlife traveled across the lands and seas once smothered by glaciers and ice. But the woolly mammoth, short-faced bear and steppe bison eventually disappeared. These giant beasts were unable to adapt to the warming climate, and humans may have hunted them to extinction. A hundred years ago, the musk ox was nearly wiped out by fur hunters. A law passed in 1917 has protected the musk ox in Canada, and they now number at least 100 000.

A SEA OF ICE

Arctic sea ice is mostly pack ice, or ice that is cracked and broken into floes that jostle and pile against one another. Pack ice constantly groans and moves.

Arctic sea ice freezes in stages. The first stage covers the sea like a thin, dark film of oil. Over one winter, it grows up to 2 m (6 ft.) thick and turns white. Ice that is more than two years old, called multiyear ice, is bluish, grows up to 4 m (12 ft.) thick and loses its salty seawater taste.

For millennia, arctic people have hunted in the pack ice and know how treacherous it is. Small boats can be punctured by shards of ice or crushed by moving floes. Sledding on pack ice is no safer — ice ridges shift, gaps of open water appear, and large floes snap off and drift away. In the Bering Strait, when a Yupik hunter failed to return from the sea ice, his wife would hang a pair of his boots outside and watch them. If they stopped swinging in the wind, she knew her husband had died.

Landfast ice forms along coastlines. It doesn't join the moving pack ice, but attaches to shore.

In spring, wide cracks open in the ice, and returning whales and birds move along these "leads" toward their summer calving and nesting grounds.

Icebergs are hunks of freshwater ice — sometimes as big as very tall apartment buildings — that break off glaciers when they meet the sea. Sailing in "bergy" water is dangerous because only one-tenth of an iceberg floats above the surface. The *Titanic* sank in the North Atlantic in 1912 after hitting an iceberg that had drifted from Greenland.

Polynyas — areas of open seawater surrounded by ice — are formed when strong winds and currents keep the water from freezing. A frigid mist of sea smoke often hangs over them. Most polynyas are small and narrow, but the North Water polynya between Greenland and Canada's Ellesmere Island may be bigger than any lake on Earth. Overwintering animals, such as walrus, beluga whales, bearded seals and some seabirds, depend on the open water of polynyas.

Ice Escapade

Norwegian explorer Fridtjof Nansen and Captain Otto Sverdrup proved that pack ice circles clockwise around the North Pole. In 1893, they sailed the *Fram* north of the De Long Islands off Siberia until it wedged into the ice. After three years drifting with the pack, Sverdrup steered the *Fram* safely into the Greenland Sea.

13

THE ARCTIC LANDSCAPE

You are standing in a valley on a remote Siberian island well north of the tree line. It is midwinter and snow blankets the ground. A few rocks and shrubs break the flatness of the valley floor — but no trees. Low mountains rise in the distance and, since the daytime moon is bright, you can just make out brown patches where the wind has blown several peaks bare.

You sense that giant forces shaped this land and understand why people think it's barren. But underfoot, the tundra is alive even when frozen solid. The ground beneath the tundra, called permafrost, holds strange powers and secrets that can change the face of the land above.

Giant Works

Many arctic valleys and plains were gouged and carved by ancient, slow-moving glaciers. Rocks are still scarred from the rubbing ice, and the soil that was scraped off has yet to be replaced. In parts of the Arctic, the land remains a rocky desert.

When the glaciers melted, they dropped their scrapings in piles. Erratics, or stand-alone boulders, look as if they were dumped onto today's landscape. Gravel ridges, called eskers, which were once meltwater tunnels inside huge glaciers, now snake across the arctic plain.

Today, some of the largest rivers on Earth flow into the Arctic Ocean. With spring melt, the Lena, Ob, Yenisey, Mackenzie and other rivers carve canyons and wash flatlands as they rush north.

Landmarks

Travelers can easily lose their way because the land looks the same in all directions. Ancient peoples of Arctic North America piled rocks into giant *inuksuit,* which served as

ELDER TALES

Old northern legends tell of giants who live in the remotest reaches of the Arctic. In some stories, the giants, when asleep, become landforms whose feet, legs, chests and faces can be seen in distant hills.

wordless signposts. Explorers erected stone cairns to mark caches of supplies or written messages.

Permafrost Power

Permafrost is ground that stays frozen year-round. In some places, it is hundreds of meters (or yards) deep and thousands of years old. The top layer, often less than a meter (about 2 feet) thick, usually thaws in summer.

Wherever the permafrost surface regularly thaws and refreezes, the land heaves and cracks. Tiny ice crystals work into the cracks. Over time, giant patterns form on the surface of the land. In places, the ice builds into huge hill-sized cores, called pingos, which jut through the permafrost and rise above the surrounding plain.

The top permafrost layer melts in June. The meltwater collects in puddles and does not drain away because the subsoil stays frozen.

Plants, insects and even some amphibians live in the wetlands on the permafrost surface. Antifreeze-like chemicals in their bodies keep their vital organs alive through the winter. Some insects hatch one summer, overwinter as larvae and emerge as adults the following summer.

Pingo

Death in the Arctic

Whatever dies in the Arctic and is not eaten right away may take years to decompose. A body kept above ground can dry out before it rots, and a body buried in the permafrost may be preserved for centuries.

In 1972 in Qilakitsoq, local Greenlanders found what they thought was a doll in a rock cave. It turned out to be the body of a baby who had died about 500 years ago. His skin, hair and clothing had been mummified by the drying wind and cold temperatures.

In 1984, Canadian anthropologist Owen Beattie unearthed the body of John Torrington — a member of John Franklin's doomed arctic expedition — from a permafrost grave near Baffin Island. Torrington's body and clothing were just as they had been when he died in 1846.

WHAT GROWS UP NORTH?

When spring arrives in the Far North, it brings 24-hour sunlight and temperatures over 2°C (35°F). The arctic tundra bursts into color as the first plants and shrubs bloom in sheltered valleys and along rocky fiords.

Despite all the ice and snow, most of the Arctic is as dry as a desert. The soil is thin and poor. Glaciers and rivers carry away topsoil, and cold temperatures slow down the decay of plant and animal material that helps create new topsoil. Although the growing season is only 60 days long, more than 900 types of plants have adapted to life in the Far North.

Mountain avens

Wooly lousewort

Purple mountain saxifrage

Arctic poppies

Lichens

Rough and brittle or soft and spongy, lichens cling to rock or trees. As they grow, lichens slowly break down rock, turning it into soil. Able to live in extremely cold temperatures, lichens are nutritious food for caribou and for travelers lost in the wild. Some Northerners add lichens to soups, breads and puddings.

Survival Tactics

- Many plants, such as mountain avens, grow in rounded clumps close to the ground, where the temperature is higher and winds swoop up and over them.
- Fine hairs on the stems and leaves of the wooly lousewort trap the sun's heat.
- The flowers of the arctic poppy act like solar collectors, following the sun all day long.

- Arctic plants, such as the purple mountain saxifrage, have tough, shallow roots that grow down into the permafrost and then spread out.
- Arctic plants pop up in sheltered spots. Dark-colored rocks attract and hold the sun's heat, warming the surrounding soil, sometimes up to 30°C (86°F).

Evergreen Tree Line

Conifers, or evergreens, form the jagged tree-line fringe where tundra ends and boreal forest begins. To survive, large deciduous trees need 120 days each year with the temperature above 10°C (50°F), but conifers only need 30 days.

Coniferous trees are shaped to survive arctic weather. The tops of fir and spruce are narrow and sharp so snow slides off without harming the branches beneath. On the windy side of trees, the branches dry out and die. With branches growing on only one side, like flags on a pole, these trees look aerodynamic.

Dwarf Trees

North of the tree line, dwarf birch, willow and black spruce are common. They are similar to their southern cousins, but grow close to the ground — almost like a ground cover. While their trunks are tiny, their seeds and cones can be a normal size. A full-grown arctic tree that is as tall as your ankles may be hundreds of years old.

Plentiful Berries

Crowberries, cloudberries, bearberries, bilberries and cranberries nourish many of the North's creatures. The high sugar content of the berries increases after the first frost, providing valuable energy.

Grasses

Grasses do well on the wet or dry tundra, where little else grows. They thrive in areas where the soil has been disturbed by heaving permafrost, retreating glaciers and grinding ice. Grasses help stop soil erosion and are excellent food for wildlife.

ECO WATCH

Windblown sulfur dioxide gas from the chimneys of industry all over the world falls to Earth in acid rain and snow. In Arctic Europe, the acid level in rivers is high enough to kill mayflies, brown trout and snails. Arctic plant life near the nickel and copper smelters of the Kola Peninsula and Noril'sk, Siberia, is completely destroyed.

ARCTIC BIRDS

It's spring in the Far North. As millions of birds arrive from the south, clouds of insects swarm over ponds and puddles. These insects are tasty meals for birds after their long migration flights.

Why is the Arctic such an attractive destination for birds? For three short months, the Arctic offers perfect conditions for raising their young — food, space and moderate temperatures.

All species of arctic birds lay and incubate their eggs and raise their young in the shortest possible time. Spring blizzards and early fall storms can kill both adults and their young. The abundant food supply vanishes when freeze-up arrives, and migration begins with the first sign of cold weather. By October, only the few year-round residents of the Far North remain.

ARCTIC TRAVELERS

Thick-billed murres

Early Arrival

Eager nesters, such as black ducks and longspurs, arrive as the ice melts and insects hatch. They stay from spring until fall.

Simple Nests

Most arctic birds make simple nests on the ground, on cliff ledges or in low bushes. Old-squaw ducks prefer nesting near arctic terns because the terns aggressively defend the whole territory from intruders.

Clever Eggs

The eggs of thick-billed murres are laid on cliff ledges. They are designed to roll in circles and not fall off. Most eggs of arctic birds are speckled and blend in with their surroundings.

Plentiful Food

The menu includes billions of insects, tiny freshwater creatures and small marine organisms — from mosquitoes to fish. Shrimp are the main source of food for ducks, terns, guillemots and gulls.

Air Miles

More than 90% of arctic nesters migrate. Some species fly east or west to open sea and hop south to the tree line, or fly all the way to South America and beyond. The others winter somewhere in between. Arctic terns make the longest flight, nesting in the Arctic and wintering in the Antarctic. Scientists think their migration pattern hasn't changed since the last ice age.

YEAR-ROUND RESIDENTS

Only a few kinds of birds live year-round at the top of the world. These tough creatures are specially adapted to cold weather and a limited food supply.

Snowy Owls

Snowy owls range from the tree line to the ice near the North Pole. Perching on top of tundra hummocks, they survey their territory and wait patiently for prey. Their keen ears can detect rodents under the snow. They eat five to ten lemmings a day, but when lemmings are scarce, many snowy owls migrate south in search of food. They also eat other birds, as well as dead fish and foxes. Thick, hollow white feathers — speckled with brown in females and their young — provide perfect camouflage and insulation. Unlike most owls, snowy owls see equally well night and day.

Ptarmigan

During breeding season, the black, brown and white feathers of ptarmigan blend into their surroundings. As the days get shorter, summer plumage is replaced with off-white feathers, making ptarmigan hard to spot against the snow. Ptarmigan are insulated against the cold by the downy feathers that cover their bodies, from their nostrils down to their feet.

Ravens

The black feathers of the raven provide little camouflage, but they absorb all possible heat. Ravens are the first arctic birds to nest each spring, usually in the middle of seabird colonies. Clever and adaptable, ravens eat fish guts, bird eggs, garbage and animal carcasses.

LAND MAMMALS

The arctic habitat doesn't suit many species of mammals, but the creatures that do live in the North are specially equipped. Some migrate or burrow into thin soil or snow. Others hibernate or change color. Some mammals survive because of their huge size. Others survive because of their huge numbers. Only 50 of Earth's 4000 mammal species live in the Far North. If one species falters, there can be a ripple effect throughout an arctic food web.

An Arctic Food Web

Fulmar

Long-tailed jaegar

Snowy owl

Rough-legged hawk

Arctic fox

Lemming

Wolverine

Ermine

LEMMINGS

Many northern animals eat lemmings or other species that eat lemmings. These chubby rodents start breeding when they are a few weeks old and give birth to three or four litters in one summer (up to 40 young lemmings a year). When their underground burrows — where they spend seven months of the year — become overcrowded, the lemmings burst out and run wildly in all directions, looking for food. Many die of starvation, exposure or exhaustion, leaving their predators hungry, too.

ELDER TALES

Hundreds of years ago, Norse and Inuit people said that lemmings dropped out of the sky. The Inuit word for the white winter coat of the collared lemming is *kilangmiutak*, which means "that which falls from the sky."

CARIBOU

The caribou, or reindeer, is a circumpolar member of the deer family whose body is built for travel in northern climates. Each spring, instinct calls all caribou back to their birthplace. Individuals and small groups join enormous herds (one herd was estimated at 800 000 caribou). They leave their sheltered wintering grounds and take the shortest path over the tundra to the calving grounds of their ancestors. Pipelines, roads and swollen rivers can confuse them and disrupt their migration. When the days of late summer become shorter, the caribou head south again.

- Caribou grow a new rack of antlers every year. Males clash antlers in bloody battles during mating season in the fall. Female caribou are the only female deer that have antlers.

- Long stiff guard hairs growing over inner fur help keep the skin extra warm.

- A caribou's brain contains a mental map of the herd's migration route.

- In summer, caribou lose up to 2 L (about 2 qt.) of blood a week to thirsty insects.

- An insect called a nose bot lays its eggs in the caribou's nose. When the eggs hatch, the larvae feed on the caribou's nose.

- In summer, warble flies burrow holes in the caribou's skin.

- Leg bone and tendon rub together, making a clicking sound that helps keep the herd together in a blizzard.

- Caribou milk is rich — 20% fat — and the young grow rapidly. Europeans milk reindeer like cows.

- Caribou can spot the slightest movement of most predators from great distances.

- Local people use the sinew of tendons as thread and as string in cat's cradle games.

- Large hooves designed for swimming and digging up snow also act like snowshoes.

- Special air sacs under the skin keep caribou afloat when swimming.

THE WELL-ADAPTED POLAR BEAR

Before the ice ages, there were no polar bears. The retreating ice isolated a small group of brown (grizzly) bears. Over time, brown fur turned to white, short necks stretched longer for easier swimming, and teeth became jagged and sharper for ripping flesh. The *ursus maritimus* ("sea bear") is now completely at home in water, on ice or on land.

Excellent predators, polar bears are the most respected and feared creatures of the North. Standing about 2.4 m (8 ft.) tall, they are oddly humanlike, sometimes walking upright and hunting the same foods as people. Native spiritual leaders, or shamans, often have the polar bear as their *tornaq*, or spiritual guardian.

Bear Facts

- Polar bears follow their noses to the snow dens of ringed seals. They break through the roof and feast on plump seal pups. Ringed seals are their favorite food, but they also devour dead whales, young polar bears, waterfowl, crabs, rodents, berries, garbage and sometimes humans.

- With their white fur, polar bears stalk their prey unseen. While waiting by a seal's breathing hole, a bear sometimes covers its black nose with a paw.

- When food is scarce, body functions slow down. Polar bears may even stop eliminating urine and feces. The growth of a fertilized egg in a female may be delayed until she is properly nourished.

- Treaded for better traction on ice and hairy for warmth, a polar bear's paw is about the size of a dinner plate.

- The largest polar bear ever weighed was 800 kg (1764 lb.). The oldest lived about 32 years.

- Polar bears can swim up to 130 km (80 mi.) nonstop. They can sprint up to 40 km/h (25 m.p.h.).

- Polar bears detect the smell of humans from up to 30 km (18 mi.) away. Humans and wolves are their only enemies.

- Thick fur holds in body heat. Hairs are hollow for better insulation and transparent so the sun's rays can warm the black skin underneath.

ECO WATCH
Polar bears hunt seals on frozen pack ice. But global warming is causing the pack ice to thin and retreat, making their hunting more difficult. Recent studies link global warming to weight loss in polar bears.

Family Life

Polar bears mate in spring. In late fall, pregnant females dig into snow dens and give birth to twin or triplet cubs. Polar bear milk is 35% fat. That's the equivalent of heavy whipping cream. In March, mothers and cubs take to the sea ice and fatten up on seals. Cubs usually stay with their mothers for more than two years.

SPECIALIZED SPECIES

Polar bears share their frozen larder with a handful of year-round residents.

Arctic Foxes

Small and hardy scavengers, arctic foxes shadow polar bears so they can feast on their leftovers. White in winter, brown in summer, they have hairy feet for warmth and traction.

Wolves

Hunting in packs, arctic and tundra wolves follow caribou and musk ox, preying on the weak and young. They also eat arctic hares.

Arctic Hares

These vegetarians live among rocks in large or small family groups. They change color seasonally and have smaller ears and bigger feet than other hares.

SEA CREATURES

Arctic sea mammals thrive in cold water. They swim, dive and bash through thick ice or laze around on a floe without getting so much as a goosebump. The sea mammals of the Arctic all have thick skin and a layer of blubber that insulates them from the cold. Bowhead whales and walrus are one-third blubber, belugas are a little more and ringed seals are half blubber. Seals also have waterproof fur that is so thick the cold water never touches their skin.

• When belugas dive, they stay under the water for 12 to 15 minutes. Their main food is arctic cod, but they also search for worms, clams and small fish in shallow or deep water. Belugas use clicking noises in echolocation to help them navigate in murky water and to communicate with other pod members.

• In water as deep as 215 m (about 700 ft.), bowheads sieve tiny crustaceans — about 50 000 a minute — through the baleen plates in their mouths.

• Adult bowheads are up to 18 m (60 ft.) long — about the length of four pickup trucks — and weigh as much as 68 000 kg (about 150 000 lb.). Their tail flukes — tip to tip — can span 7 m (23 ft.).

• Bowhead nostrils are located high on top of their heads so they can breathe easily through the smallest crack in the ice.

Natural Enemies

Some scientists believe that belugas and bowheads choose migration routes and feeding grounds to avoid killer whales. True arctic whale species lack a dorsal fin, allowing them to swim in ice and break open breathing holes from underneath. Killer whales' massive dorsal fins force them to stay in open water.

Overhunting

Overhunting during the nineteenth century, mostly by southerners, drastically reduced sea mammal numbers. European and American whalers killed thousands of bowhead whales for their rich oil and plentiful baleen (used in making corsets and umbrellas). Scientists wonder if bowhead numbers will ever recover. Belugas were hunted by Native whalers for their blubber, which was used for lamp oil, and for their skins, which were used for making boats.

The ivory tusks of walrus were carved into tips for billiard cues. Their hides were made into bicycle seats and rope. Today, walrus are not hunted commercially, but dredging for clams in the Bering Strait disrupts their feeding grounds.

• Walrus rake the sea floor as deep as 91 m (about 300 ft.) below the surface, using their prickly whiskers to locate clams, sea cucumbers and other bottom-dwelling crustaceans. Some eat ringed seals.

• When walrus dive, blood moves from their skin to their inner organs. Their skin turns white in freezing water and changes back to a pinkish brown when they pull themselves onto a floe to rest.

REINDEER HERDERS

When the ice age glaciers finally melted, seals, walrus and whales swam into the newly opened arctic seas. Herds of reindeer, or caribou, grazed on the greening tundra. Hardy hunting peoples, mostly from central Asia, followed the animals north and became the first settlers of arctic regions of Europe and Asia.

With the tree line well above the Arctic Circle in Europe and Siberia, hunters could track reindeer onto their summer tundra pastures, then retreat to the trees in winter and stock up on wood for fuel, tent poles and tools. But even with a wood fire, arctic winters are bitterly cold. The settlers invented their own survival gear, and they learned to herd reindeer. For thousands of years, the herding way of life continued, and many ancient inventions were in daily use.

The Early Saami

Early Saami people of Arctic Sweden, Norway, Finland and the Kola Peninsula fished in rivers and the sea, hunted elk and bear, and herded reindeer. For winter travel, they invented skis and fur boots that were bound onto skis. To make and break camp quickly, the Saami used a portable skin tent called a *kata*. The bowed wood frame provided maximum headroom, crossbars to hang cooking pots over a central fire and a hole for smoke to escape. The Saami also invented a unique one-person, one-runner sled, or *pulkka*, that was harnessed to a reindeer. Two-runner cargo sleds, or *reki*, were pulled by several reindeer.

ARCTIC SETTLEMENT IN EUROPE & ASIA

20 000 years ago	10 000 years ago	7000 years ago	5000 years ago
The ice age covers much of the Arctic, but eastern Siberia remains glacier-free. Ancient mammoth and reindeer hunters camp near the Indigirka River.	The ice age ends, and hunters settle the Far North. Soon they begin to use captured reindeer as live decoys to lure and kill wild reindeer.	The dogsled is invented in Siberia.	Tool making improves as arctic peoples begin to flake stones into tiny, razor-sharp microblades.

The Ancient Evenki

The ancient Evenki of Siberia bred and milked the largest reindeer — animals so sturdy that people rode on their shoulders. They didn't like to kill their own so they hunted wild ones for meat and skins. They caught fish in traps woven from branches. The Evenki designed thigh-high deerskin boots, stuffed with dry grass, to keep warm in the deep snows of Siberian winters. They lived in large conical tents, called *chums,* covered with reindeer skins.

The Early Nganasan

The early Nganasan fished and hunted wild reindeer, geese and ducks on the coastal tundra of north-central Siberia. They traveled on small reindeer-drawn sleds, venturing below the tree line to collect wood to make tent poles and sleds. The Nganasan preferred white-furred deer for making parkas, which they decorated with dark fur. Their boots were full-length leggings with roomy, puffy feet.

ARCTIC SETTLEMENT IN EUROPE & ASIA

4000 to 2000 years ago	1100 years ago	800 years ago	400 to 300 years ago
Families start corralling and feeding small herds of reindeer. Herders in Sweden use ski sticks to dig in the snow to help their reindeer find lichen.	Norway's King Ottar demands taxes from the Saami — to be paid in reindeer hides, bird feathers and walrus skins.	Russian fur traders start moving northeast. Contact with Native people living in the Arctic becomes more frequent.	The Nenets and Saami begin mass reindeer herding. In search of pasture above and below the tree line, they partly follow and partly lead the huge reindeer herds.

EARLY ARCTIC HUNTERS

During the last ice age, hunters from Asia crossed the Bering land bridge into glacier-free parts of Alaska and Canada's Yukon. When the ice age ended, Asians continued to move into Alaska, but then they turned south. For 5000 years, no people lived in the treeless parts of Arctic North America, Greenland and even northeastern Siberia, but animals thrived, especially along the coasts.

The Paleo-Eskimos

The Paleo-Eskimos were the first people to settle the barren coasts of North America and the Bering Sea. They came from Siberia carrying bows and arrows and microblades. Finally, people had tools strong and sharp enough for them to survive without wood. They were able to create a way of life using arctic materials, such as stone, moss, sod, bone, antler, sinew, hides and fur.

inuksuit

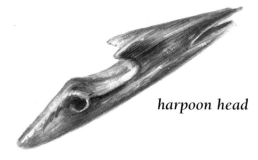

harpoon head

The Dorset

Descendants of Paleo-Eskimos, the Dorset people had no sturdy boats, but learned to hunt seals and walrus from the ice edge. Wearing notched-bone ice creepers on their feet to dig into ice, they threw harpoons with barbed blades that hooked under the skin and blubber of their prey. The Dorset people probably invented the snow house, which they kept warm with soapstone lamps filled with seal oil burning on a moss wick. They built rock weirs in rivers to trap fish and clustered groups of rock statues, called *inuksuit,* to direct caribou into ambushes.

The Thule

Eventually, people living by the Bering Sea invented seaworthy, multi-person skin boats called *umiaks* and improved the one-person kayak. Their descendants, the Thule, carved ivory and bone harpoon heads that twisted sideways under an animal's skin. They attached inflated sealskins, or *avataqs,* to their harpoon lines to slow down wounded prey. These inventions made it possible to hunt large whales offshore. The Thule also designed the *ulu,* a knife women used to cut up whale meat.

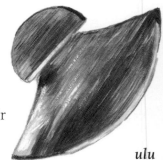

ulu

ARCTIC SETTLEMENT IN NORTH AMERICA & THE BERING SEA

24 000 years ago	10 000 years ago	4000 years ago	2500 years ago
Ice age hunters live in the glacier-free northwest, including the Bluefish Caves near Old Crow in Canada's Yukon.	The last ice age ends.	Paleo-Eskimos move into the eastern Siberian and North American Arctic.	The Dorset culture emerges as the Paleo-Eskimo culture fades.

The Early Inupiat

The early Inupiat people, descendants of the Thule in northern Alaska, lived along the migration route of the bowhead whale. A whale chase in skin boats was dangerous, but a successful kill brought in huge amounts of food. Where whales were plentiful, people settled in sod-covered village homes. Hunters wasted little of the bowhead. Families feasted on *muktuk* (a delicacy of raw skin and blubber) and shared the meat with their sled dogs. Whale oil fueled lamps. Jawbones were used for tent poles and sled runners and baleen for nets and snares. The Inupiat hunted other animals as well, but whaling was the heart of community life.

The Early Inuit

The early Inuit, also Thule descendants, lived in isolated family groups in the eastern Arctic. They hunted whales when they could, but they mostly fished, netted birds and hunted caribou inland and seals along the sea ice. Whole families followed the hunt. They camped along the way in snow houses or tents and cached surplus meat for hungry times. The Inuit used a fan harness with ivory hitches for their dog teams. It spread out the weight of dogs and cargo so hunters could speed safely across thin ice.

ARCTIC SETTLEMENT IN NORTH AMERICA & THE BERING SEA

2500 to 2000 years ago	1200 years ago	800 years ago	400 to 300 years ago
Bering Sea peoples develop a boat-building and whaling culture.	Thule whalers sail north into arctic waters. The Dorset people disappear, possibly killed by the advancing Thule.	Norse settlers in Greenland meet the Thule.	The Arctic turns colder. In most places, hunters cannot depend on whaling and turn to mixed hunting.

TRADITIONAL BELIEFS

Ancient arctic people lived far apart and spoke many languages, but they shared deep-felt beliefs. One belief was that all natural objects and living things have spirits and must be treated with respect. They believed that people called shamans had remarkable powers. Energized by dance and drumbeat, the shaman's soul could fly to the spirit world and negotiate with the spirits to help control weather, heal the sick, find food animals and even harm enemies.

Traditional Siberian shaman with staff and drum

Was the legend of Santa Claus inspired by stories of shaman flights and reindeer-drawn sleighs?

Early arctic people passed along their beliefs through stories. This version of the well-known Inuit legend of Sedna, the sea goddess, dramatizes how spirits and shamans have powers to help, harm and change ordinary people.

Sedna, the Sea Spirit

Sedna lived with her old father on an island. She loved to comb her beautiful hair. Many men admired her, but she refused to marry them.

One day a stranger paddled his kayak to the island. "Come with me and I promise you great riches," he sang to Sedna. "Your pot will always be full of meat, your lamp filled with oil, your bed covered in soft skins and your clothes lined with warm feathers."

Sedna could not resist the stranger's song. She agreed to marry him. On their voyage to his home, the stranger transformed himself into a fulmar — a spirit bird with mystical powers. He flew Sedna high over the sea and dropped her on a rocky ledge. Every day the fulmar visited her, carrying a meal of fish guts in his beak.

In her loneliness, Sedna cried out for her father. "Father if you knew my suffering, you would rescue me from this terrible place."

When spring came, Sedna's father decided to find his daughter's home. After many days paddling his kayak, he reached the rock ledge. When he saw his daughter's misery, the old man was so angry that he killed the fulmar. Sedna jumped into her father's kayak, and they paddled quickly away.

But other fulmars found their dead brother and chased after the fleeing kayak. Sedna heard their wailing and called, "Oh, Father, we are followed. What shall we do?"

The old man pushed Sedna into the bottom of the boat and covered her with skins. He paddled so fast his kayak skimmed over the waves. The fulmars swooped low, trying to hit the old man with their stiff wings. He struck back with his paddle. Then the fulmars hit the sea with their wings, beating the waves into a terrible storm.

Waves washed over the kayak, and the old man was desperately afraid. He threw Sedna overboard, but she clung to the side of the kayak. The old man grabbed his knife and stabbed at her hands, cutting off each finger at the first joint. The bloody pieces, bobbing in the sea, turned into the first seals. Sedna again grabbed the kayak, but her father cut off her fingers at the second joint. These pieces turned into the first walrus. Then, when Sedna clutched the edge of the kayak with her bleeding stumps, her father cut off her hands. They fell into the water and became the first whales.

Sedna sank to the bottom of the sea but did not drown. Instead, she became a spirit who jealously guards her sea creatures. But without fingers, she can't keep her hair from getting tangled. At times it bothers her so much that she won't release animals for people to eat until a shaman visits and gently combs out her hair.

EXPLORERS, WHALERS AND TRADERS

About 500 years ago, Europeans began making expeditions into the Arctic. Many lost fingers, toes and feet to frostbite before returning home. Others froze to death. Some died clutching silk handkerchiefs, fine teacups and bedroom slippers, which they had tucked into their bags to remind them of a gentler life at home. But people kept heading back to the North, searching for new lands, furs, gold, whales and adventure.

From 1550 to 1820, most Arctic expeditions were looking for a northeast or northwest sea route from Europe to the riches of India and China. But it wasn't until 1879 that Adolf Nordenskjold of Sweden sailed through the Northeast Passage, and 1906 that Roald Amundsen of Norway finally sailed through the Northwest Passage.

1 Near Iceland, 520 — Brendan and 17 fellow Irish monks stare in wonder at icebergs from their curragh, a wood-framed boat covered with ox hides.

2 Greenland, 987 — Eric the Red, a Norseman banished from Iceland for two murders, starts a farming colony that lasts 500 years.

3 Frobisher Bay, 1585 — England's Martin Frobisher thinks he has found gold, a unicorn's horn and a channel to Asia. They turn out to be fool's gold, a narwhal tusk and a bay on Baffin Island.

4 Davis Strait, 1587 — England's John Davis keeps a record of the lands and peoples he visits using his new invention — the ship's log.

5 Kara Sea, 1596 — Willem Barents's Dutch ship is crushed by ice. The crew treks to land, but Barents dies of scurvy on the way.

6 James Bay, 1611 — Mutineers set Henry Hudson, his young son and seven crew members adrift in an open boat. They disappear without a trace.

Northwest Passage

Northeast Passage

Whalers and Fur Traders

Unlike most explorers, European and American whalers and fur traders overwintered in the Arctic and had regular contact with people there.

Europeans hunted whales off Svalbard in the early 1600s, and then in the Davis and Bering Straits, where Americans joined the hunt.

The whalers not only hunted the bowhead to near-extinction, but also introduced fatal diseases, such as polio, diptheria and smallpox, to northern communities.

Traders moved north overland and by river, setting up trading posts and collecting furs from local trappers. Below the tree line, the most prized furs were Siberian sable, Pacific sea otter and North American beaver. Above the tree line, traders preferred arctic fox and seal pelts. The sea otter and sable were severely overhunted. When fur sales dropped in the south, the trappers suffered. Many had come to rely on cash and guns from traders.

(7) Gulf of Anadyr, 1648 — Russian fur trader Simon Dezhnev probably sails through the Bering Strait — before it is named.

(8) East Siberian Sea, 1728 — Vitus Bering, a Dane employed by Peter the Great of Russia, sails north through the Bering Strait, into the Siberian Sea, verifying that Asia and America are not connected.

(9) Cape Dezhnev, 1824 — Ferdinand von Wrangel finishes mapping the north coast of Siberia for Russia.

(10) Victoria Strait, 1847–48 — Sir John Franklin and 128 men die of lead poisoning from eating tinned food during their second winter stuck in ice. Search parties for the lost ships map much of the Canadian Arctic.

(11) Laptev Sea, 1881 — American George De Long discovers the New Siberian Islands and then dies when his ship is crushed in the ice. (8)

SOUTH MOVES NORTH

Early explorers, whalers and fur traders searched for adventure and riches in the Arctic, and then they returned home. But early in the twentieth century, a few southerners started moving to the Far North — this time to live and work.

Arctic peoples had never worried about borders between countries. But in the 1920s with the discovery of natural resources in the Far North, governments began to draw lines in the ice. They sent police into northern communities to enforce national laws. Mining and oil companies staked out claims and developed gold, diamond and drilling operations. During World War II, the military moved in.

The southerners who settled in the Far North brought schools, stores, churches and medical clinics. They also brought a plentiful supply of alcohol, as well as cigarettes, junk food and eventually TVs. The southern lifestyle changed northern communities forever. For Northerners, some changes were good and some were bad.

Roads and Resources

- During World War II, the Alaska Highway was built, connecting Alaska to the rest of the United States.

- From 1928 to 1953, prisoners in Siberian labor camps built roads and railways to new mines and hydroelectric projects.

- In the 1970s, tankers laden with oil began to chug through pristine arctic waters. Environmentalists and hunters held their breath — every oil spill would be a human and wildlife disaster.

- When waterways freeze in winter, ice roads and bridges connect some communities and industries. It's risky work driving huge rigs over frozen lakes, but specially trained drivers are paid high wages.

Military Invasion

Airstrips were built in Canada, Svalbard and Greenland during World War II. Used for refueling planes, some of these sites became larger, permanent settlements, such as Thule, Greenland. Americans and Russians patrolled the sea ice of the Arctic Ocean with submarines. Deadly nuclear material from abandoned, obsolete submarines and weapons now pollute Russian arctic waters.

In 1954, Canada and the United States decided to construct the DEW (Distance Early Warning) Line — a chain of radar stations stretching from Alaska to Greenland that would warn of a Russian air attack.

Equipment and military personnel were shipped north through the Mackenzie River Delta.

Local people were hired as construction workers, many of them earning cash for the first time. The military has now abandoned these sites, but it has left behind heaps of garbage, used equipment and toxic waste.

Military planes still head to the Far North to practice low-level flying maneuvers, which seriously disturb both people and wildlife.

Snowmobiles and ATVs

By the middle of the 1960s, snowmobiles had transformed winter travel in the Far North. Ten years later, all-terrain vehicles (ATVs) had changed summer travel. Most Inuit hunters and Saami herders own a snowmobile and ATV. Hunters can cover a larger area with a snow-mobile. That means that some animals, including the wolf, may be threatened by overhunting. In some areas, ATVs roaring around on the tundra damage the sensitive surface layers — perhaps for decades.

NENETS HERDERS

Most descendants of reindeer-herding peoples live and work in towns while their children attend school. At home, they try to maintain their ancestral customs, stories and language. But when families no longer live on the land, traditional ways can be quickly lost.

Several hundred Saami and Nenets families remain on the land, following the ways of their ancestors. They're still connected to the modern world and use conveniences such as snowmobiles, digital watches and shortwave radios. But they work hard to balance a healthy traditional life with modern culture. Their lifestyle gives meaning to important traditions and is a source of pride to relatives living far from home.

In northern Siberia, Katya's family lives a traditional life with eight other Nenets families, their dogs and a herd of 4000 reindeer. The whole group — people, animals and gear — is called a brigade.

Each family in the brigade eats and sleeps in a *chum,* a huge tent made of 60 reindeer skins on a frame of spruce poles. In Katya's *chum,* reindeer skins cover the plank floor and a woodburning stove warms the inside. Oil lanterns light the *chum* on dark days and glow warmly on the tent walls at night. For meals, the family sits on cushions around a short-legged table. Katya curls up on a pile of soft reindeer skins to sleep.

On summer days and inside the *chum,* Katya wears a sweater and jeans. But in winter, she pulls on her reindeer-skin coat, or *yagushka,* and the boots her grandmother sewed by hand and lined with reindeer fur.

Each year in late winter, the families in the brigade pack all their belongings into reindeer-skin bags and load them on wooden sleighs.

Each sleigh is harnessed to several reindeer and lined up in a long caravan. With the sleighs ahead of the herd, the brigade trudges 1000 km (620 mi.) north.

Families make camp every night and break camp every morning until they reach tundra pastures in early spring on the Yamal Peninsula. The reindeer must cross the Ob River while it is still frozen and reach the tundra before their calves are born.

At the end of each day, the men tend the reindeer while the women assemble the *chums*, set up the stoves and make reindeer stew for supper. Katya usually collects moss and birch shavings for toilet paper and diapers. She feeds the family's Samoyed dogs and helps tend any sick or wounded reindeer.

Summer brings welcome changes. The reindeer grow fat grazing on the tundra. Older children return home from boarding school. The family sleeps in a summer tent and cooks on an outdoor fire fueled with brush willow. Katya picks cloudberries and helps prepare char netted in streams and lakes. The family visits sacred sites on the Yamal, leaving gifts of antler and fur and saying prayers for the sick.

In early fall, the brigade starts the trek south to the shelter of trees near the Arctic Circle. This time, the reindeer, some still pulling sleighs, swim across the Ob River.

ECO WATCH
Radioactive cesium, released during the nuclear accident at Chernobyl in the Ukraine in 1986, traveled more than 2000 km (1200 miles) west and contaminated the lichen eaten by Saami reindeer. Many Saami herders had trouble selling their reindeer meat for 10 years.

INUIT HUNTERS

A modern hunter reads the waters, land and weather like a well-loved story. He almost always knows where he is and what's going on. He notices unusual details and can predict what lies ahead. This ability to read the natural world comes from traditional knowledge passed on from the elders and from personal experience. Because Inuit hunting families must keep moving to find food, their knowledge covers all sorts of conditions over vast areas of northern Canada or Greenland.

For much of the twentieth century, the Canadian government forced Inuit children to attend residential schools far from home. They were not at home to live and learn a hunting life from their elders. Today, few Inuit hunt full-time, but many hunt at least part of the year.

Joshua was born in an outpost camp. He is learning traditional skills that tell him when the sea ice is safe for travel, where to find fresh seabird eggs, which way a polar bear will charge and much more. But he also likes to snowmobile to town for supplies where he can listen to rock music and surf the Internet.

When hunting, Joshua's family travels light. All equipment sits on a sled pulled behind a snowmobile or a team of husky dogs. With only a snow knife and a pattern in his mind, Joshua can build a snow house, or *iglu*, in a few hours. He finds the kind of snow he needs, cuts and places each block in a spiral, and forms a windproof dome.

In summer and early fall, Joshua and his family travel inland to fish and hunt caribou. At the beginning of winter, they join other families on the sea ice to hunt seals. In spring, the families scatter for more sealing, netting birds and catching fish.

When hunting ringed seal, Joshua searches out their breathing holes in the ice. Like a polar bear, he crouches beside a hole, not moving a muscle, until the surface of the water moves. Then he throws his spear or shoots his gun to kill the seal before it senses him and dives back under the ice.

After a successful hunt, the family butchers and shares the meat and fat. Some meat is dried and cached under rocks for later use. Skins are scraped and worked until they are soft enough to sew. With caribou, the sinew from tendons is peeled off bones and used as string.

Most meat is eaten raw or stewed. Sometimes walrus are

stuffed with birds and left to age in seal oil. Berries, roots, leaves and even poppy flowers are eaten when available. Meat, fat and fish prepared in the traditional Inuit way provide a nourishing diet — even without fruits and vegetables.

Back to the Land

In the late 1960s, some Canadian Inuit worried that their culture would disappear if everyone lived in settlements with TV, store-bought food and alcohol. A small back-to-the-land movement was born, and the government helped willing families set up outpost camps. There are now more than 50 such camps in the Canadian Arctic.

ECO WATCH

Dangerous chemicals from the south, including PCBs and pesticides, travel north and fall in the Arctic in snow, rain or dust particles.

Toxic metals from smelters in Noril'sk and the Kola Peninsula slowly circulate around the North. These pollutants enter the food chain and are eaten by people who eat wild foods. Is it fair that pollution from half a world away is poisoning the traditional foods of Inuit families?

INUPIAT WHALERS

For 300 years, outsiders overhunted the bowhead whale. By 1930, when it became illegal to hunt them, there were not enough bowheads left to count on for food anymore. Today, the whales and whaling cultures are at risk.

Inupiat, Yupik, Chukchi and Inuit people still hunt a limited number of bowhead whales. Each year, scientists and elders help decide where and how many can be hunted. It's a hard decision because there are so few whales left. About 7500 bowheads spend the summer in the Beaufort Sea, and many fewer live in the eastern Canadian Arctic.

A Modern Whale Hunt

On the north coast of Alaska, a modern Inupiat whaling team is made up of the captain, or *umialik,* a harpooner and crew. Today, most *umialiks* do not rely on skin boats. Instead, metal boats are rowed by the crew or powered by outboard motors. The whaling crews may also have high-tech radar systems on board.

Umialiks used to build clubhouses, or *karigi,* for their crew to prepare for the hunt. Today, young Inupiat men train all winter and take strength and endurance tests with older crew members in the community center. After working out, seasoned hunters share stories of past hunts, the treacheries of pack ice and how to survive when lost. Some modern hunters paint old-style pictures of the whale or carve detailed miniatures of hunting parties. Newspaper and magazine photos of past hunts hang on the walls of the community center.

Inupiat elders believe that if a hunter is respectful, the bowhead will let itself be caught. All equipment is carefully cleaned so as not to offend the whale. Traditionally, women sewed new white-skin outer shirts for the whalers. Today, the men usually wear sweatshirts bearing the crew's logo under their high-tech survival suits and life jackets.

When flocks of snow buntings return in spring, *umialiks* know it's time to pull the boats to the beach and set a whale watch. Hunters look for good weather and a whale close to shore. If a whale takes too long to tow in, it may sink and become a wasted "stinker."

When a bowhead is sighted, several boats head to where it last appeared, wait and then rush to where it resurfaces. The hunters usually harpoon the whale first and attach it to floats. In the past, they killed the weakened whale with lances. Today, they may throw a ceremonial lance before using a "bomb gun." Then they attach more floats and tow the whale home. As they tow the whale to the beach, the crew often sings traditional songs to help lighten their load.

The successful *umialik* is the one whose harpoon makes the first strike. On shore, his wife greets the whale with fresh water. After the whale is hauled in, the *muktuk* and meat are cut off and shared with the whole village and sent to relatives living in distant places. Scientists gather around, excited by the chance to study a bowhead up close.

The community celebrates with feasting, storytelling, singing and games, including the popular blanket toss from a walrus hide.

ECO WATCH
Animal rights activists and traditional whalers have conflicting beliefs about hunting bowheads. Are animal rights more important than the rights of people to live the way they have lived for thousands of years?

LIFE IN A MODERN TOWN

Wild terrain, long distances and fierce weather isolate most northern communities. But even in remote villages, there are kids going to school, playing with friends and watching videos. Despite the isolation, most northern kids do the same things that kids do all over the world — with a little help from technology.

Education

Most northern kids go to school in their own communities. Children living in very remote regions attend boarding schools and return home for summer and holidays. Many northern kids are taught in their traditional languages. Some schools are equipped with computers, which hook students into the World Wide Web. The University of the Arctic, centered in Rovaniemi, Finland, is a university "without walls." Students take classes by computer hookup and earn degrees without leaving home.

Groceries

A head of lettuce may travel a great distance — by air or land — before it ends up on a family table in the North. Transportation costs make most food items three to four times more expensive than in the south. Hunting and fishing not only save money, but also provide Northerners with traditional foods.

Agriculture

To get around the high cost of shipping in fresh foods, some Northerners have tried growing their own fruits and vegetables. Greenhouses are experimental in Greenland and northern Canada. In Noril'sk, Siberia, a successful farmer sells milk from her herd of cows and fresh cucumbers and onions from her greenhouses.

Health Services

Most health problems are looked after close to home. Small communities have nursing stations, and larger ones have a resident doctor. Some larger communities have hospitals. People with complicated diseases are flown to large urban hospitals in the south.

Technology

Advanced computer technology makes it possible for a Toronto heart specialist to examine a sick child in Nunavut, with the help of a trained nurse, phone lines and a video camera. A special stethoscope sends the child's heartbeats to the doctor's ears. That beats a seven-hour air flight to a hospital far from home!

Housing

Houses built on permafrost are prefabricated wooden structures with sloped metal roofs and oil furnaces. Heat from buildings melts permafrost, causing foundations to shift and crack. To keep the ground cold and houses upright, buildings are raised up on blocks, stilts or gravel.

Highrises

In large towns in Greenland and Siberia, apartment buildings have been constructed above the permafrost, with varying success. Some of the older buildings have slumped over or are slowly sinking into the ground.

Utilities

Because of the permafrost, water pipes and electric wires cannot be buried. Some communities run pipes and wires through heavily insulated tubes called utilidors, which are laid on or above the ground and heated in winter to prevent freezing. Electricity and telephone poles are planted in gravel inside large metal cylinders.

Garbage

Empty oil barrels and piles of garbage are an ugly reminder that waste cannot be buried and little rots in the North.

Recreation

Recreation centers throughout the Arctic offer hockey, volleyball, table tennis and badminton competitions. In summer, northern kids take advantage of good weather and long days. Games of soccer and baseball are played after midnight, when light allows. In Greenland, seal ball — a sealskin ball stuffed with grass — was played long before basketball arrived from the south.

TRADITIONAL ARTS

Carving and needlework — using natural materials — have always been important traditional arts of the Native peoples of the Far North. A creature carved from a walrus tusk or a mitten hand-sewn from a reindeer hide grows out of the heart and hands of an individual artist. But each piece of art also preserves a culture's rich traditional knowledge. As Native elders are teaching young people carving and sewing skills, they are also sharing an understanding of the stories and the symbols that are expressed in their works of art.

The Art of Carving

In the past, northern peoples carved everyday tools with such skill that the tools are now valued as works of art. Today's carvers, still working in stone, bone and wood, create pieces of art to sell to collectors. Their works often show the respect they have for the spirit world and shamans, as well as for the natural world and the traditions of their people.

In a traditional game, young Yupik girls tell each other stories and illustrate them by drawing scenes and characters on patches of mud or snow with a beautifully carved story knife.

Saami people carve wooden items, such as these spoons, with intricate designs that date back to ancient times.

Today, Inuit stone carvers capture the strong feelings at the center of their stories in the stark poses of their hunters, spirits and animals.

The early Dorset people were master carvers of bone and tusk. Their works have a haunting beauty. The lines on this bear's back suggest its skeleton or arteries.

The Art of Fur and Skin

When a hunter wears fur and skin clothes and then stalks a caribou, or reindeer, he looks like the animal he's hunting. Arctic legends tell of people who actually transform into animals and animals that turn into people. Some older parka designs from Canada's Baffin Island had tails sewn on the back and small ears on the hood.

For many traditional peoples, such as the Nganasan of Siberia, clothing designs were sacred gifts from the spirit world. They had to choose their clothing carefully. For the Inupiat, it was disrespectful to wear clothes made from land-animal skins when hunting sea animals, and vice versa. Today, fur clothes are still charged with meaning for the makers and are sewn as works of art.

An Inuit mother's parka has a wide hood, or *amaut*. Her baby can ride naked in there — safe, warm and peeking out.

The Yupik people have traditionally made waterproof anoraks out of walrus guts. These remarkable windbreakers keep sailors warm on bitter, damp days.

Inupiat women are known for making dolls and dressing them in tiny traditional parkas, perfect in every detail.

Drums, made from animal gut stretched across a frame, vibrate with the power of shamans all over the North. Drummers beat the rim with a stick or turn the drum from side to side, thumping it with their wrists or a stick.

INTO THE FUTURE

The people of the Far North are determined to pass on to their children a healthy environment and a love of the land. Together, they are cooperating as neighbors and communities to protect this beautiful but harsh place they call home. At the same time, Northerners are celebrating their rich cultures and preserving traditional ways.

Protecting the Environment

Arctic people know it's up to them to protect their natural environment. At circumpolar meetings, they have developed plans to solve problems that threaten the environment, such as oil spills in arctic waters, toxic wastes piled up at abandoned industrial and military sites, and pollution coming from other parts of the world.

Though there is still much more to do, some progress has been made in protecting the Arctic for future generations. In 1997, Russia created the Nenetsky Nature Reserve, where large areas of tundra and coast were set aside as breeding grounds for walrus, spawning rivers for fish and nesting sites for birds. And wind- and solar-power stations are being built along the Murmansk coast to provide a source of clean energy to one of Russia's most polluted regions.

ECO WATCH

The Norwegian government wants to protect Bear Island, home to one of the world's largest seabird colonies. But this special wilderness borders on oil deposits. Will it be nature reserve or oil field?

Celebrating Cultures

The people who live at the top of the world enjoy getting together to celebrate life in the North. One of their favorite events is the Arctic Winter Games. Held every two years in a different arctic community, these games are the "Olympics of the North." Through the long, dark winter, young athletes practice traditional Inuit sports that are played inside an *iglu*, such as the high kick, arm pull and knuckle hop. Drummers, throat-singers and dancers also spend the winter practicing for their parts in the games' opening and closing ceremonies. In March, when daylight is returning, the games bring a welcome break from winter, although spring may still be months away. Winners take home *ulu*-shaped medals. And everyone takes home happy memories.

Self-Government

On April 1, 1999, the Inuit of the eastern Canadian Arctic proudly celebrated the creation of Nunavut, a vast new territory that they now govern. Some of the North's Native people have already settled land claims and self-government agreements. Others continue to negotiate, believing that important decisions about the North should be made by the people who live in the North.

Images of the Arctic

About 50 years ago, Inuit artists first learned to spread inks on their block carvings to make prints. Today, many printmakers and carvers sell their bold images of arctic life worldwide. Through art, they share with southerners the dreams and realities of their amazing arctic world.

INDEX